THE HORSE WHISPERER

AN ILLUSTRATED COMPANION TO THE MAJOR MOTION PICTURE

THE HORSE

AN ILLUSTRATED COMPANION

PHOTOGRAPHS BY

JAY DUSARD, JOHN KELLY, ELLIOTT MARKS,
KEN REGAN, AND BARBARA VAN CLEVE

WHISPERER
TO THE MAJOR MOTION PICTURE

FOREWORD BY ROBERT REDFORD

TEXT BY GRETEL EHRLICH

BANTAM PRESS

LONDON • NEW YORK • TORONTO • SYDNEY • AUCKLAND

£3

TRANSWORLD PUBLISHERS LTD
61-63 Uxbridge Road, London W5 5SA

TRANSWORLD PUBLISHERS (AUSTRALIA) PTY LTD
15-25 Helles Avenue, Moorebank, NSW 2170

TRANSWORLD PUBLISHERS (NZ) LTD
3 William Pickering Drive, Albany, Auckland

Published 1998 by Bantam Press
a division of Transword Publishers Ltd

A catalogue record for this book is available from the British Library.

ISBN: 0593 044711

Printed in the United States of America

CONTENTS

FOREWORD

We live in an age of information domination. Much of it perhaps is not needed or necessary. It may be an old-fashioned notion, but I would prefer to call personal discovery the most defining mark of a project. For that reason, I shrink from the idea of explaining too much with the hope that the film will speak best for itself.

Apart from that, here are a few issues that provoke me and have abided my interest most of my life: the real West versus the mythological West of film and fashion fiction. The real West today is mostly real estate entrepreneurship and a declining lifestyle related to ranching and family life. The old West was always inhabited by a large population of homesteaders and outlaws and held hostage by a few hundred barons.

I like what's left of nature and its seasons—the sweet smell of October as leaves of summer die and the air is still. The quiet fall of snow and its quilting of the frost-hardened landscape. The raw, bone-breaking winds that gather speed across what is left of the open plains. The distant and lonely sound of the midnight truck on the highway. The flush of new color in spring and sounds of water and stock as it all comes to life. I love the stories told by those that live and work there, will die there and know it. The hard-lived, often brutally treated anecdotes around the corral fence or campfire that mitigates against the reality of fate in such a wide open and unpredictable space. The rituals of hat, leather and rope that define the aristocracy that remains. And the remains themselves—those few ranches that are not prefaced with the phrase "view sites" or "estates." Those dusty, rutted dirt roads not yet paved. The waters that still flow freely undisturbed by the "know better" hounds of industry. The air so pure, it seems out of place.

Aside from that, this story struck me as being just that—a good story with interesting characters in growth and conflict, about a new approach to the age-old connection between man and beast. One that involves trust and compassion. The circle seemed to complete itself with the idea that that approach need not be exclusive to animals alone.

Adapting this novel meant working in this landscape, but by way of math. A great percentage of filmmaking is math, which means reducing a novel's spacious framework for its art to a manageable, watchable length. Making story and character work in a more confined format inevitably means making difficult choices and sacrifices. The novel allows for time to reflect and digest while reading, where film, by definition, must move inexorably ahead without pause.

Previous spread: Redford as Tom Booker brings a horse to Annie Maclean, played by Kristin Scott Thomas. The ride that follows features beautiful footage of the Montana landscape. Inset: Tom Booker and brother Frank, played by Chris Cooper, repair a barbed wire fence on their ranch, the Double Divide.

As a director, Redford was very specific about the visual aspects of the film. As is shown below, he would often look through the camera himself to be certain the image was just what he had in mind.

The scrims shown above were used to create the appropriate lighting for a crucial scene in the movie between Redford's character, Tom Booker, and Annie, played by Kristin Scott Thomas.

Opposite: Pilgrim tries his hand at directing.

THE WEST

There is a fundamental need in all of us to move out from under tyrannies, whether political, emotional, or economic, imposed from the outside or from within. We have to eat and breathe; we have to make peace with ourselves and society. The western frontier was a physical answer to the need for space. It represented what Wallace Stegner called "a geography of hope." *The Horse Whisperer,* filmed on location in Montana, draws directly on this "geography of hope" as it tells the story of the healing of a young girl, her family, and a broken horse. The West's breaks and draws, dry gulches, hanging alpine lakes, red-walled mesas, towering cirques, strings of cottonwoods following streams roaring out of the mountains, still carry with them the possibility of a fresh start and a path toward basic sanity. The West was once described as "a place of great breathing." Its open spaces, both real and metaphorical, are essential to life itself.

In *The Log of a Cowboy,* written in 1902, a foreman gave this advice to the young men on their first day trailing cattle from Texas to Montana: "Boys, the secret of trailing cattle is never to let your herd know that they are under restraint."

The West was once wide enough to move trail herds that way. Cowboys could string out a bunch of cattle farther than the eye could see, and keep going that way for five months without hitting a single strand of barbed wire. It was also a place where a man or woman could move out from under the conventional orthodoxies of thought, shedding oppressions and falsehoods— all those dictatorships of the soul—and set about breathing in fresh air.

Liberation, as that Texas foreman understood a hundred years ago, is not a single geographical point on a map but a pact agreed upon, an internal tension between discipline and chaos, because that's the only way freedom can occur. Yet to ride a good horse behind a herd of cattle at dawn at the beginning of summer in the high country can go a long way in showing us the way to this state of mind; to live in a community where you are judged on how ardently you pitch in, how willing you are to get the work done with patience and respect, how easily you can laugh at yourself—that is what living in the West can be.

There are no more frontiers. But there is still a West. You can find it on the map and run your finger down its eastern edge: in the North Dakota grasslands on both sides of the Little Missouri River where Theodore Roosevelt ranched between 1884 and 1886; the Black Hills of South Dakota, the Sand Hills of western Nebraska, the Flint Hills of western Kansas—still unplowed and rich in native prairie grasses—and slicing down through Oklahoma's panhandle into the hill country of Texas. Sweeping west from there are the rich grasslands of southern Arizona and New Mexico, and arid mountains where black panthers still roam; then up the Rocky Mountain cordillera that begins in Durango, Mexico, and stretches far north into Alberta and the Northwest Territories. Great sweeping plains fan out to the east from the Rockies, and on the west side of the Continental Divide, range after range of mountains lie down and flatten out into great basins, then are gathered up again—as if a big hand were grabbing and pulling the land back into peaks—all the way to the Pacific Ocean.

Henry David Thoreau once remarked that he wished his neighbors were wilder. He would have loved the West, because even in its current subdivided, eviscerated state, it still has great pockets of wild lands and a feral exuberance that cannot be restrained; vestiges of the West's former freedoms still inspire, still work on the tired mind as a healing balm.

The view from most western ranches goes for at least a hundred miles. Because of the vast landscape we've inherited, Americans, especially westerners, are prone to loneliness. The nearest neighbor may be ten or twenty miles away, and town fifty or a hundred miles—a bend in the road with a bar, a half-stocked grocery store, a gas pump, and nothing more. Living well on a ranch is the art of making do. The cowboy's life has stood for the achievements of individual humans, grasses, sun, and animals, not masses of humans and the machine.

Living on a ranch, undisciplined needs are curbed; it's a place not only for renewal but for invention: ranchers are frugal—they make what they need, cook the foods they long for, entertain themselves with storytelling, dances, pack trips, cookouts, or just plain howling with the coyotes.

To understand this place, wherever it is—north or south, desert or alpine, sand hills or rock faces—you have to put in some time. A ranch is not a plaything to be purchased like a car or visited only when the weather is good. Rural life demands and engenders constancy: land is time; time is metered out in snowfall, wind, drought, floods, and blizzards. Rewards come only to those who stay through all the seasons. That means every day, all day, because there are no shortcuts to intimacy.

A ranch is a miniature society. A generosity is implied; there's room enough for everyone: families and hermits, alcoholics and churchgoers, cowboys and bankers, the old and the young, the brilliant and the slow-witted. And it's necessary, like it or not, to find a way to all get along. Isolation provokes a feeling of closeness and gives rise to tolerance; when you see a pickup coming down the highway, you slow down to talk, share a thermos of coffee, or at least a wave. Neighborliness is a prerequisite, a moral imperative. You can't not respond when someone is in need.

Ranchers and cowboys are famous for their dry wit and intractability. But they also stand for togetherness and community, though these might be invisible from the road if you're driving by.

Community consists of animals—working dogs and saddle horses, herds of sheep and cattle—and a motley crew of people on whom they are dependent

Production Designer Jon Hutman and his team of carpenters built the ranch house, pictured at right, from scratch. This house, which served as the Booker family home in the movie, was very close to a real house or "practical"— a set that is a real establishment.

The picture at right shows Annie Maclean's car approaching the ranch for the first time in the movie. As you can see, the set was suffering from run-off from the rivers in the area full from the recent spring thaw. Sand bags were used to protect the relatively perfunctory foundation of the ranch house.

and who are dependent on them. The young men who rode north from Texas with the trail herds quickly learned that cowboying requires impeccable teamwork. When moving cattle, you are assigned positions by the boss: you ride point, flank, or drag. A good hand anticipates when things are about to go wrong, and makes sure he is there in the right place at the right time to catch the pieces. If a young horse is about to start bucking, a rider will come alongside to give the colt confidence; if the calves are turning back and running down the mountain, a rider will back off a little to catch them when they come.

The image of a cowboy loping off alone into the sunset is infrequently seen. Usually, it's the whole crew, riding four or five abreast, eagerly anticipating a drink of something cool back at the ranch and a long sleep after dinner.

Neighbors always did and still do help each other brand, turn out, and gather cattle in the spring and fall of the year. They also help at any other time, with a sick child, a horse caught in a bog, a fence that needs repairing. A fine thread binds everyone to everyone else. If you ride out alone to check cattle, your neighbor will call in the evening to make sure you have returned home. If there's a blizzard, a death, a birth, an accident, everyone helps out. Sympathy notes aren't written—you show up to give a hand doing chores. Ranching communities, no matter how far-flung, form a network of relatedness. Like it or not, you are part of the skein. There are feuds, hotly contested opinions, and a complete lack of anonymity. You are known, loved, hated, but most of all tolerated. The individual *I* is replaced with a collective *I*—one that contains howls, whinnies, moos, wind songs and snowy silences, the song of the meadowlark and the evening song of the robin. Rugged individualists beware: You are all in it together.

The myth of the American cowboy is a stale idea, and good hands on a ranch are neither macho, thick-skinned, nor violent. The owners of the Double Divide Ranch, where *The Horse Whisperer* was filmed, describe their father as "hardhanded but fair."

If a cowboy looks gruff it's because his lips are too chapped to permit a smile; if he takes a deep seat on a frosty morning it's because he's been bucked off four or five times on the previous day and he's sore. Can a cowboy be replaced by motorcycles and helicopters? "Hell no. You can't abuse those things the way you can abuse a cowboy," one veteran told me. Life in the saddle means you are someone to whom everything happens: you're rained on and snowed on, struck by lightning, bucked and fallen with, and given almost no pay for regular fourteen-hour days.

Ranchers are inextricably linked to family, in the largest sense of the word. It goes beyond wives, husbands, and children; family means encompassing all living things. A rancher's work is wholly taken up by breeding, birthing, and nurturing, by putting water on native hay fields, and watching calves, lambs, foals, and puppies being born. The best of these ranchers are providers and protectors; they live and die within the extended families of animals, sage-grass communities, townspeople, and livestock tenders. A cowboy is more midwife than tough guy, and a natural tenderheartedness goes with the profession. How could it not? It is humbling work. Nature's violent strokes leave scars that confirm one's insignificance, and heroism comes in odd forms: by being resourceful, keenly observant, and undaunted by hard work and solitude.

If western men have been wrongly stereotyped, then, in most accounts,

Hutman added old wood to an already existing shacklike structure to create the Creek House where Annie and Grace Maclean stay while at the Double Divide.

women haven't been mentioned at all. Historically their importance in the West is obvious: They have been the bearers of education, culture, and civilization, of political equality and fairness, of temperance and extravagant living; of morality and amorality. They were pioneer wives bouncing across the Oregon Trail in wagons; they were gun bank robbers and gun toters, schoolteachers who married ranchers and rustlers; they were horse thieves and justices of the peace, political organizers and suffragettes, actresses and gold-rush prostitutes, writers and diarists, rodeo performers and stage drivers dressed as men, captives who joined their Native American captors' tribes, and Mormons who pushed handcarts west on their own Mormon Trail, only to be sent north by Brigham Young as "colonists" to Idaho and Wyoming. Their stories are wonderful to read.

These days, ranch women ride and rope, fix fences, irrigate, work the calving shed, train colts, work as veterinarians and cattle foremen, herd sheep, and ride the rodeo circuit, as well as doing domestic chores: cooking, caring for children, keeping the books. In other words, ranch women often take on a double workload.

The extended family of a ranching community includes a variety of work crews: there are men or women who ranch alone, as well as husband-and-wife teams, teams of siblings, or a foremen with a crew of riders who might live during the summer in isolated line camps, cow camps, or sheep wagons. It's not a glamorous life. Perhaps the idea of an antihero is more descriptive of what a cowboy or rancher is. At the end of a long season of moving herds, doctoring calves, searching for strays, and weathering storms, it's not a hero's accolade they want, only a few laughs over an iced tea or a whiskey.

Everything we think of as "western" originated in Mexico. The Spaniards first introduced cattle and sheep to Mexico, which they called "New Spain." Because the animals prospered and multiplied, and rustlers began taking what animals they wanted, the cattle soon needed to be tended. Many Spaniards, among them priests who oversaw the cattle belonging to the missions, thought such work was beneath them and so they sought workers from among their converts—the Native Americans, African Americans from the West Indies. These men became known as *vaqueros*—from *vaca*, "cow"—the forefathers of the American cowboy.

The vaquero was in no way a romantic figure. Day work as a laborer on horseback was thought to be one of the lowliest jobs around. Where it was sunny and brushy they wore wide-brimmed *sombreros* to keep the sun and sudden afternoon downpours off their faces. They wore cotton shirts and pants from fabric made by the Aztecs, and in winter, wool shirts spun from the merino sheep introduced by Mexico's first viceroy. The rest was made from leather, which they often tanned, cut, and sewed themelves. The poor, sixteenth-century vaquero wore leather *chaquetas* (jackets), leather pants or *botas* (leggings).

Annie Maclean discovers Tom Booker, played by Redford, Frank Booker, played by Chris Cooper, and Frank's son Joe, played by Ty Hillman, working with a calf in a small corral when she comes to the ranch to find her "horse whisperer."

Because cowboy boots as we know them had not yet been made, and even if they had, the vaqueros could not have afforded them, they often went barefoot.

Perhaps the earliest piece of cowboy equipment was the spur, thought to have originated in 700 B.C. and worn by horsemen in Mesopotamia and southern Europe. The vaqueros' spurs had large rowls that jingled when they walked, even though they were, at first, strapped only to the cowboy's bare ankles.

Living with the herds in the sixteenth century meant living like animals: the vaquero slept under the stars on a piece of cowhide, since ranchers did not provide bunkhouses. It must be remembered that the word *hacienda* comes from the root word *hacer,* meaning "to do" or "to make." The *hacienda* was not a home, but a place where work was done.

In seventeenth-century Mexico, the number of cattle and wild horses increased so greatly that one onlooker described their presence as "a spectacle to the eyes, animals everywhere you looked." Individual ranchers might own as many as 130,000 head of cattle and and raise 30,000 calves each year. Bulls weren't castrated, nor were the horses the vaqueros used, so the daily work of tending herds was wild and often dangerous. Many animals became feral. Ten- and twenty-year-old bulls that had never had dealings with humans attacked vaqueros and their horses while resisting capture. Yearly roundups were established and the word *rodeo* came into use from the Spanish *rodear,* meaning "to go around."

The Spaniards brought the *silla de montar* saddle from Old Spain, but developed the working saddle in the West Indies. When vaqueros started using *reatas*—ropes with slipknots—to rope cattle in the 1700s and 1800s as they moved north into California and New Mexico, they first tied the end of the rope to the horse's tail. Dangerous and inhumane, this practice was soon modified by the addition of the saddle horn. What we know as dally roping (seen in team roping events at a rodeo) was invented by the vaqueros in California. The word *dally* is coined from *dé la vuelta,* meaning "to turn around," alluding to the practice of wrapping the lariat around the saddle horn.

The Spanish government sent Franciscan priests and soldiers to build presidios and establish missions up and down the Californian coast. The vaqueros moved north with their sheep, cattle, and horses, trailing livestock all the way from Zacatecas, Durango, San Luis Potosi, Santa Barbara, Querétaro, and

Curt Pate, a trainer on the film, works with Pet, technical advisor Buck Brannaman's horse, and one of the stand-ins for Pilgrim, in a small round corral under a particularly spectacular Montana sky.

Guadalajara: to New Mexico in 1598, Texas in 1690, California in 1769. The cattle were longhorns—smart, resourceful, and superbly adapted to arid lands with little water, a variety of predators, and a short feed supply. By 1774, there were approximately 25,000 head of cattle in Texas; by 1842, the herd number had risen into the hundreds of thousands; by 1860 there were an estimated 4,500,000 cattle on the Texas range alone.

Soon enough it wasn't only vaqueros on the range. In the 1840s there was a flood of emigrants from the East and Midwest who crossed the Oregon and Mormon trails to get to the gold rush and the promised lands of Utah, Oregon, and California. The Civil War changed the demographics of the West. Confederate soldiers who had returned home to find their farms in ruins moved westward from the Deep South, looking for a new start and for freedom, as did the freed slaves. African-American cowboys and southern boys lived and worked together and thrived in Texas. At the same time, the booming industrial cities of the North increased the demand for meat and hides. A steer that could be bought for four dollars a head in the West could be sold for thirty dollars in Illinois. The cowboys hired on at newly formed ranches or created ones of their own. The Mexican and southwestern U- or L-shaped adobe ranch house was replaced by eastern architectural styles. In Kansas, pioneers first lived in little round-backed, dirt-floored sod houses, or else clapboard saltbox or simple Victorian houses with ample porches made from imported wood. On the northern ranges, where pine forests abounded, the log cabin was reinvented from its origins in Pennsylvania. The log roofs had sod on top, where cacti and grass grew in summer. Mud was used for chinking the cracks between hand-hewn logs. The roofline was low and a tall man had to stoop to get in the door. Besides the house, there might be a bunkhouse, a set of corrals, and a saddle shed—simple shelter, nothing more. The spirit of the stone and adobe hacienda in Mexico as place of "doing" and "making" remained.

The demand for beef cattle vacillated. Then something happened that changed western life. On May 10, 1869, Leland Stanford swung his sledgehammer, missed, and swung again until he hit the golden spike in Promontory, Utah, signaling the completion of the Transcontinental Railroad. This meant that the western states were not only open to cattle and open-range ranching, but also to commerce. The railroad galvanized ranching into an industry.

Thousands of cowboys moved millions of cattle up vast networks of trails; north from San Antonio on the Chisholm Trail to Abilene, Ellsworth, and

Redford rides out into the landscape.

Dodge City, Kansas; west on the fifteen-hundred-mile-long California Trail from El Paso through New Mexico and Arizona, to the large ranches that spread up and down the coast of California, from burgeoning Los Angeles to what would become the gold-rush town of San Francisco, into the northern Rockies on the Goodnight-Loving Trail straight north into Colorado and Wyoming to Miles City, Montana, or following the Yellowstone River straight west to Bozeman——on an offshoot called the Bozeman Trail. On December 3, 1866, after a 2,500-mile journey, Nelson Story and his cowboys trailed the first longhorn cattle from Texas into the Gallatin Valley, not far from where *The Horse Whisperer* was filmed. Shortly thereafter, the Bozeman Trail, which had brought them to Montana, was closed because the danger from Native Americans was deemed too great. It would be another twenty years before the overwhelming impact of cattle and cowboys was felt on the northern range.

There was one cowboy for every 150 to 300 head of cattle; the trail herd

Redford and Scarlett Johansson, who plays Grace Maclean, in the back of Booker's truck, a '77 Ford pick-up bought from a couple in the local town of Livingston, Montana.

numbered anywhere between 1,500 to 3,000. Each rider had seven to ten mounts, a fresh horse for every day of the week, roped out of the remuda before dawn. A scout rode ahead and looked for crossings and suitable overnight spots, and a camp cook set up his oxcart or chuck wagon to prepare meals. What one European king, Charles II, had called "the naked land"—i.e., the American West—was now swarming.

The West was described in one diary as a great body, an unwieldy giant, an earth-bound Jonah—muscled, graceful, and heaving with storms—which one rode. The land was nothing if not varied, encompassing Sonoran and Chihuahuan deserts, short and tall grass prairies, oak savannahs, lodge pole pine forests, cedar breaks and red-earthed draws, desert mountains and alpine cordilleras, great basins of arid sage-grasslands studded with prairie cacti and greasewood flats. Much of the West looked like the moon, what Jack London called "an aching, eye-hurting desolation." For some, such as Theodore Roosevelt, who had been severly asthmatic as a child, the outdoor life was a necessity. In 1884 he fled the East Coast following political defeat and tragedy: His wife of four years had died in childbirth and his mother had succumbed shortly afterward. He founded a ranch under the bend of the Little Missouri River, in North Dakota, and later recalled those few years as the best of his life.

Livestock and people were on the move for two decades, from the 1860s through the 1880s. To the novelist

Dianne Wiest plays Frank's wife, Diane, a typical ranch wife. Wiest modeled much of her character after Marie Engle of the Engle family ranch, where much of the movie was shot. Here she moves some hay—just one of the many chores in a day on the ranch.

At right, Marie and Keith Engle of the Engle family ranch, where the movie was shot. Keith is one of five brothers and sisters of a family who has been ranching for generations.

Director of Photography Robert Richardson against the awesome backdrop of the West he worked hard to capture in *The Horse Whisperer.* An award-winning director of photography, he received an Academy Award® for his work on Oliver Stone's *JFK.*

Producer Patrick Markey, pictured at right with co-producer and first assistant director Joe Reidy and below with fellow producer Redford, has a special appreciation for the Montana landscape. He has had a home in nearby Livingston, Montana, for years.

Willa Cather, who grew up on the Nebraska prairie, it seemed as if the whole world were running. Cattle and horses were pastured in common everywhere. The public land was open, the use of the range free for the taking. Nothing about overgrazing was yet understood. With no fences, the Mexican longhorns ran wild.

The American cowboy began to be seen as a folk hero, a man of the earth who went fast, had style, and possessed a spirited moral fortitude that lacked the Puritan prissiness and self-hatred. The open spaces of the cowboy's West didn't belittle him—after all, he was horseback. Rather, it fueled him with daring and exuberance and a self-effacing sense of fun.

There was also tedium and exasperation to the work. Living with the herds could be devastatingly hard and dangerous. An old cowboy song called "The Kansas Line" set the scene:

Technical advisor Buck Brannaman shows off some of his best rope tricks.

A good rope is never far from the side of any true cowboy.

Ty Hillman, who plays Joe Booker, was discovered for the role through the Colorado Junior Rodeo Association. He spent much of his downtime on the set mastering new rope tricks learned from Brannaman and Cliff McLaughlin. At top, he shows an appreciative Redford what he has learned.

Come all you jolly cowmen, don't you want to go
Way up on the Kansas line?
Where you whoop up the cattle from morning till night
All out in the midnight rain.

The cowboy's life is a dreadful life,
He's driven through heat and cold;
I'm almost froze with the water on my clothes,
A-ridin' through heat and cold.

As cowboys moved into the northern plains they met up with English breeds of cattle that had been brought to America by the colonists, then west to Illinois, Iowa, and Missouri, and on to Kansas, Nebraska, and the Dakotas. These were shorthorns, Durhams, and Herefords, among others, and interbreeding between the long-legged, resourceful longhorns and the beefier but more fragile English breeds began taking place.

The way the cowboys dressed changed with the cold climate. The cotton shirts and pants of the vaquero were traded in for buckskin pants, or wool shirts, pants, and vests bought at army posts along the way. They tied two-foot-square bandanas of linen, cotton, or silk loosely around their necks for warmth, pulling them up over their mouths while sorting cattle in dusty corrals. Other uses for the neckerchief were as tourniquets, napkins, bandages, snot rags, and head scarves with which to tie down their hats on windy days.

When the spring and fall rains came, and the winters that could drop snow

as early as September and last until April, the cowboy inherited blanket-lined canvas coats, long split-tail slickers for rainy weather, and for winter riding, the buffalo robe—an ankle-length coat made of buffalo hide and cowhide, as well as horsehair. When it was really cold, they might wear all three.

The cow towns in Kansas, Nebraska, Wyoming, the Dakotas, and Montana, where the Texas longhorns were delivered, were robust and vital centers. The cowboys were paid in cash, and after four or five months on the trail with little sleep and often miserable conditions, they celebrated. The soulful campfire songs of the lonely cowboy were given over to theatrical events. In the bigger towns served by railroads, there were plays, concerts, lectures, the occasional circus, and variety theaters with "men only" performances. Legitimate drama and opera were less well received. One Laramie, Wyoming, newsman described his first operatic music experience as "sitting upon our ears and stomachs about as delightfully as the midnight singing of a jackass."

From left, Steve Conard, a featured extra and wrangler on the film, Don Edwards, who plays Smokey, and Guy Small, another wrangler on the film. These accomplished horsemen helped move cattle and worked in the branding scene.

Buffalo Bill and his troupe performed "Major Cody" and "Lost and Won," and old ballads were sometimes sung whose roots could be found in both Spanish songs and southern folksongs, such as "The Last Rose of Summer," "The Old Log Cabin," and "Way Down upon the Suwannee River."

Dancing was always popular in Wyoming and Montana, where most folks didn't observe religious restrictions on having fun. Out in small communities, diaries from the late 1880s describe long journeys to a dance hall by spring wagon, buckboard, or horseback, bringing food and drink, and children, who slept in bedrolls by the side of the dance floor. Dances lasted all night. Breakfast was cooked in the morning and sometimes the dancing continued.

Coming to town meant personal hygiene was attended to: a bath, then a haircut and shave, and a new set of clothes amply provided by the town merchants, whose own backgrounds must have seemed exotic: many were Jewish

Wranglers move cattle before the branding scene.

Annie Maclean and Tom Booker move cattle into the high pasture for the summer.

Finally, the cattle head into a corral behind Tom and Frank Booker to await branding.

immigrant traders who had followed the gold rush to California by ship, then moved to the Rocky Mountains.

There were the usual entertainments: bars, gambling, prostitutes, dances, and horse races, and though the cowboys were hardened to living outdoors in every kind of weather, they took advantage of a few nights of rest in a real bed with no herd to keep watch over, before setting off on the long ride home.

Cattle and horse rustlers lived nomadically, often wintering in caves. Where Butch Cassidy and his Hole in the Wall Gang lived for a short time in eastern Wyoming, the marks their kitchen fires made are still visible on the interior walls.

Overgrazing and overcrowding of rangeland by sheep and cattle brought the downfall of the open range. The winter of 1886–87 proved the point. Winter storms laid down entire herds from Montana all the way to Texas. One rancher said that after the blizzard, he walked on the hides of his own dead animals for a hundred miles. The thirst for freedom had turned to greed and lawless-

Richardson (behind the camera) and his crew capture Redford on horseback.

ness. Granville Stuart, a pioneer Montana cattle rancher, described how quickly the open range changed:

"In 1880 the country was practically uninhabited. One could travel for miles without seeing so much as a trapper's bivouac. Thousands of buffalo darkened the rolling plains. There were deer, antelope, elk, wolves, and coyotes on every hill and in every ravine and thicket. In the whole Territory of Montana there were but two hundred fifty thousand head of cattle, including dairy cattle and work oxen.

"In the fall of 1883 there was not one buffalo remaining on the range, and

the antelope, elk, and deer were indeed scarce. In 1880 no one had heard of a cowboy 'in this niche of the woods' and Charlie Russell had made no pictures of them; but in the fall of 1883 there were six hundred thousand head of cattle on the range. The cowboy, with leather chaps, wide hats, gay handkerchiefs, clanking silver spurs, and skin-fitting high-heeled boots was no longer a novelty but had become an institution."

The need for controlling livestock and the use of grazing land, grass, and water quickly became evident. The "wire that fenced the West"—barbed wire—was also called "the devil's hatband." It was invented by Joseph Glidden in 1873 in De Kalb, Illinois, after his wife requested that he somehow fence in her rose garden. Fencing the range brought conflict and bloodshed. Groups of armed men went around at night cutting fences, and ranchers attempted to protect what was lawfully or unlawfully theirs.

With or without barbed wire, ranching and the cowboy life persisted. A life on horseback fostered contempt for machines and any labor not done from what Texas cowboy Charles Siringo described as "the hurricane deck of a Spanish pony." Later, the sentiment was expressed this way: "If it can't be done horseback, it ain't worth doing." What is referred to as a "cowboy's ranch" is one with no roads, no holding pens, and very big pastures—tens of thousands of acres or more apiece.

By the end of the century the frontier had been used up. There was no new place to go. Fences, laws, towns, roads, trains, the automobile, schools, libraries, and churches—all became a reality. Mormon pioneers came west from Illinois as religious outcasts, pushing handcarts and traveling in wagons with a few sheep, a milk cow, and a handful of young children. The communities they developed were semisocialistic: ten percent of their earnings were tithed, herds were run communally, and an in-church welfare system allowed them to provide for their own in times of sickness, accident, or disaster.

Schoolteachers rode out on stagecoaches to educate the young of isolated ranchers. Land and water use laws were adjudicated, and the absurdity of the 1862 Homestead Act was hotly contested by John Wesley Powell, who understood that public domain lands should be distributed in 2,560-acre parcels, not 160 acres, because of the aridity of the land. His proposal, called the "Report on the Lands of the Arid Region of the United States," was defeated in congress, but ranchers circumvented the restriction by amassing great quantities of homesteads, getting everyone in the area to sign up for one, then buying the plots from the unwary townspeople.

A thrilled Ty Hillman runs out from the dust of the branding. Although he's been to many real-life brandings, this was his first captured on film.

After encouragement from Tom Booker, Grace is put to work keeping the branding irons hot and actually branding cattle. Although every effort was made to ensure that the branding seemed authentic, no cattle were actually branded. It is, however, illegal *not* to brand your cattle in Montana. A representative from the American Humane Association was on hand for all the scenes that used animals.

While the invasion of the Southwest by Spaniards and their animals, with all its adventure and abuses, has had an almost five-hundred-year history, the settlement of the northern plains and Rocky Mountain states has taken place in less than a hundred years, and is still within memory. As one ninety-five-year-old Wyoming rancher exclaimed, "Isn't it a splendid thing to have had a hand in the evolution of society?"

A rancher's year in the northern Rockies, where *The Horse Whisperer* was filmed, starts in spring. Calves are born when the ground is still snow-covered, and in April or May they are branded, castrated, vaccinated, and given vitamins. Branding time is celebratory. Neighbors go from ranch to ranch helping each other. Calves are roped—headed and heeled—and everyone gets into the act of keeping the branding irons hot and giving shots. Afterward there's a feast, and the next day everyone moves on to the next ranch and the next branding.

When the grass comes in April or May the cows and calves are turned out onto spring range. Cowboys "ride fence," making repairs where necessary and keeping watch over the cattle, usually living with them in a line camp or sheep wagon. As summer comes on, the herds are slowly moved up into the mountains. By the Fourth of July, which can still be cold, the cattle and cowboys are living at 8,000 feet. Mornings on horseback are frosty. The horses buck and crow-hop, and the riders check the young calves for pneumonia, make sure the cows don't eat toxic wildflowers, and keep the bulls in close so they'll do their job.

Summer heats up and cattle gain weight quickly. Down in the valley, hay fields are irrigated, and hay is cut, baled, and stacked; kitchen gardens are planted and harvested. By the end of September, it's time for fall gathering. Depending on the size of the ranch and the roughness of the terrain, this can take a week or a month. Cows, calves, yearlings, and bulls are brought down from the high country to corrals, where they are sorted and brand-checked by inspectors, and the ones that are sold are shipped away.

The mother cows are brought back down to the valley before the snow comes in November. Once the snow stays on the ground and the grass is covered over, cattle are fed hay from wagons pulled by teams of horses or from the backs of flatbed trucks. Dark comes early. A pot of soup simmers all day on the wood cookstove. Wood is split—it takes about ten cords to heat a house in the winter. Tack and harness are mended and new tack is made. At night, books are read aloud and stories are told. There are meetings, land plans, and budgets to attend to—all the things the rancher is too busy to do in summer.

Jon Hutman, the production designer on *The Horse Whisperer*, designed and built the Double Divide ranch house, along with head carpenter Brian Markey and Terry Riley, a local consultant on historical buildings. They were also responsible for the houses, pens, and barns on the Double Divide set. Hutman

No one is left out of a branding. Here, champion roper Tammy Pate holds down a calf while Annie innoculates it before sending it back to its mother.

said, "We did a massive search in Colorado, Wyoming, and Montana first to try to find a dramatic setting for the movie, then design the houses. There is something about the combination of the drama of the mountains and the scale that you find here that's unique to Montana. It wasn't just a backdrop to the story, but in a lot of ways what the story was about."

Hutman looked at one hundred ranch houses in the area. "We wanted a very simple, classic ranch house," he said, "and a feeling that the Booker family had been attached to this land for several generations. I wanted to give the setting a reality and weight, a sense that we were seeing 'the rings of the tree'—a rich sense of history."

Brian Markey added, "We wanted to model the main house on an existing house in the area—a big, roomy family house with porches and a big kitchen, and an upstairs bedroom and study for Tom Booker. We found one—an unfrilly Victorian—and used it as our model. It was built from scratch, and all the doors and windows were made in our own mill."

From Tom Booker's bedroom in the main house, he looks down on a beautiful log cabin where Annie and Grace are staying. The creek house looks old but was actually put together from three existing homesteader cabins. Markey says, "It was a labor of love. One cabin came from White Sulphur Springs, another from down the road, and the third was a fallen-down cabin on the ranch. Once again, everything was handmade. We felt this was important, especially in the cabin, because in those days you didn't go to town and buy machined cabinets at the local Home Depot. It took us about eight months altogether to design and build the two houses, using fifteen carpenters and eight painters full-time for five months."

A June flood held up the making of the movie. Built on the edge of a creek, both houses became inundated for two weeks with water a foot deep. Markey said, "We protected the buildings with hay bales, and sandbagged them. If we hadn't, the rather provisional foundations would have given way. Water covered the cabin floor. Actually, it helped us give a weathered and worn look to the place, and we wanted that. That's how it has to be when you work on location; you try to use whatever happens. The floods definately added character."

A cowboy's gear is functional, designed to keep the elements off one's back, to protect bones from breaking, skin from the scratches of thorns, tree limbs, and barbed wire, and the head from rain, hail, and snow. In 1863, after a climb on Pikes Peak, the Philadelphian hatmaker John B. Stetson became the most famous maker of cowboy hats. The low-crowned, broad-brimmed Mexican *poblano* was transformed into the felt "Boss of the Plains" Stetson, usually off-white, sand, or pale brown, with a ribbon or horsehair hatband. Hats were also made of beaver and nutria fur. Crown heights and brim widths varied, and shaping a hat was and is a delicate process performed over a steam kettle.

The chaps—derived from the Spanish *armas* and, later, *chaparejos*—are batwing, chinks (knee-high), or shotgun (long) chaps, of elk, deer, or cowhide, sometimes with a decorative fringe or silver conchos. About *The Horse Whisperer,* master saddlemaker Chas Weldon of Billings said, "I usually don't have time to make chaps much, but for this movie I ended up doing a lot of zippered shotgun chaps, tooled belts, and tooled spur straps."

Buffalo robes aren't seen now, but long yellow split-tail slickers are rolled up on the back of every saddle and used almost daily during afternoon thunderstorms; insulated coveralls and blanket-lined coats are de rigueur.

Cowboy boots have always been a matter of pride. Bleucher, Justin,

Brannaman sets his sights on an unsuspecting calf. Traditional branding as illustrated in the film is said to be the most humane method because the procedure allows the calves to return to their mothers almost immediately.

Hyer, Tony Lama, and Nocona were boot makers from the late 1880s and continue to make boots today. The high boot, almost knee-high, fends off the bite of the rattlesnake and protects the leg from brush. The high, underslung heel keeps the foot more securely in the stirrup and prevents the foot from pushing through in case of a buck-off or horse fall. The soles of cowboy boots are thin. This allows the rider to feel the stirrup and keep the balance on the ball of the foot; or, when riding a rough string of horses, one can lock the edge of an oxbow stirrup against the boot heel, which helps to hang on when going fast. Now cowboys can be seen wearing lace-up packer boots with a fringed tongue, and ropers prefer flat-heeled Justin boots, but for the cowboy out on the range the old fear of getting "hung up in a stirrup" persists. Those who ride thirty or forty miles a day still favor the high-heeled, high-topped boot.

All silver work—bits and spurs—originated in Mexico, and the best makers of those objects now are of Latino descent. Spurs are not only functional—they send a message to the horse to turn or speed up more precisely than the blunt end of a cowboy boot, and are not, despite their looks, cruel—they can also be small, chiming works of art. The California spur was inlaid with silver, vaquero-style, with long rowls—the tiny wheels that whir at the end of the spur—and jingle-bobs attached to the pins that held the rowls in place. When these hit the spinning rowl, the spurs jingled. The Texas spur and the ones used in the North were less flamboyant. Rowls were sometimes long, sometimes short like tiny stars, and blunt-ended. Some had twenty points and some only three or four. The cruel, high-port Spanish bit is now, blessedly, being supplanted by the mild curb.

Rawhide braiding was also common on California and Nevada ranches. The hide of a cow is tanned, stretched, dried, and cut into long strips, and the pieces braided and knotted into headstalls, reins, and reatas. On one island ranch off California, where the foreman comes to town only once a year and complains that even once is too much, he and the vaqueros who work for him still make all the saddles, bridles, hackamores, and chaps used on the ranch. Buying those items from the outside is not allowed.

The saddle was always the cowboy's most prized possession, beside his horses. The thick-horned Mexican saddle underwent changes after its first appearance with Hernando Cortes. The Texans made a lightweight (twelve- to fourteen-pound), single-cinch saddle with large stirrups. The Californians modified the thick saddle horn to a skinnier one and called it the Visalia saddle. The cowboys of Wyoming added a double rigging—front and back cinches and a breast collar to better hold the saddle in place while roping. There were steel and nickel-plated saddle horns, and ones made of wood wrapped in rawhide (now rubber is used). There were also a variety of stirrups: oxbows, bentwood, iron stirrups, and ones with *tapaderos* attached to protect the rider's toes from snow and brush. Sometimes the leather work is tooled, or stamped with a basket-weave pattern, or left plain. There are long saddle strings in back to tie on a slicker, and a ring to slide a pair of hobbles or hold fencing pliers or a medicine bottle. The waiting list at Chas Weldon's shop for a saddle is three to five years. But Weldon and the movie's technical advisor Buck Brannaman designed a vaquero-style saddle for Redford to use.

The West is now almost impossible to define, so layered is it with mystique and lies, magic and devastation. The material culture of the region, in true American style, is profoundly pluralistic and multicultural. The Spanish, Mexicans, French, English, Scandinavians, Germans, Chinese, Jews, and Japanese, to name a few, were all influences. Wallace Stegner defined the West as "the native home of hope." That's what Tom Booker was counting on. But how do we find the real within the iconographic?

The Horse Whisperer gives us a view of a working ranch that has passed through one family, generation after generation. The Double Divide is a place of doing, nurturing, teaching, and learning. It is a sanctuary to come to and a nest from which the young and the newly initiated can fly free. Flying free, of course, inevitably means coming home, whether it's to the place in which you were born or to the landscape in which you feel most comfortable. In the open spaces one can still find that place. And if you give yourself to it, surrendering to its demands, limitations, and hardships, and developing what the writer Gary Snyder calls "an etiquette of the wild"—self-discipline, an open mind, and respect—it will give of itself freely in return.

THE HORSES

"The greatest misfortune is for one to lose his father when he is young or his horse during a journey."

—Mongolian proverb

The Crow Indians thought horses rose up out of dark water, fully formed, strong, supple, and black in color. The Sioux first called them *Shoon-ka wah-kon,* "wonderful dog" or "elk-dog." Before the coming of the horse it was dogs and women who carried the heavy loads. The Arikara believed that the souls of horses would punish those who had been cruel to them. There were prayers, poems, and shaman songs to horses in Mongolia, China, Greece, Egypt, and Arabia. The poet Li Po wrote:

The Horses of Heaven come out of the dens of Kushanas,
Backs formed with tiger markings, bones made for dragon wings.

The second-century Chinese emperor Wu Ti, searching for immortality, sent soldiers to the northwest reaches of his country, now Turkestan, to bring back the fabled "Heavenly Horses" that would transport him to heaven. In the sixth century B.C., Buddhism was brought across the Silk Road from India to China and Tibet atop a horse.

In mythology, horse and human became one in the form of the centaur, a primeval being descended from Hindu *ashvins,* or "horse drivers." Tibetans had a half-horse, half-man god named Hayagriva to whom prayers were directed for the protection of horses. The Norse people called their horses "all swift" and "early wakers" that pulled the sun across the sky. The Mongolians made block-print flags depicting a *kei-mori,* or "wind horse," thought to bring joy to every household.

In Greece, the mythical white horse Pegasus sprung from the cut-off head of Medusa, and equipped with wings, immediately flew to the top of a high Peloponnesian mountain. There he struck the ground with his front hooves and water came forth, flying skyward like a fountain, throwing poems into the air that came down to humans' ears like songs.

The early origins of the winged horse make sense to anyone who has ridden a horse fast in open country. Ordinary life is quickly left behind; going fast on the strong body of a horse means living freely. Long before the Greeks had horses, *Equus caballus*—the domesticated horse—was found in central Asia. In 1994, the bones of a horse with bit-marks on his teeth (meaning he had been ridden or driven) were found in the Ukraine and dated back to 4000 B.C. Early records show the domesticated horse in both China and Mesopotamia in 2000 B.C., Greece in 1700 B.C., Egypt in 1600 B.C., and India in 1500 B.C.

If horses have been venerated, worshipped, idealized, and loved for as long as humans have known them, it is for good reason. The horse has lived on this planet forty million years longer than the human and reached its evolutionary prime twenty million years before *epithacanthropus erectus,* the

Opposite: Pilgrim played here by High Tower, one of the best trick horses in Hollywood.

human who could stand. The horse is the oldest existing mammal; the human is the youngest.

The domesticated horse profoundly changed every culture it entered into. On the back of the horse, national boundaries were changed, material goods circumambulated the world, religions migrated, wars were won, other horses were stolen, hunters found game, dead souls were carried to heaven. After all, our Anglo-Saxon word *horse* comes from *hors,* meaning "swiftness." Why wouldn't we humans, then, venerate this regal animal?

The horse is now represented by only one genus, *Equus caballus,* the modern domestic horse, and one wild horse, *Equus przewalski,* found on the Gobi Desert by a Russian army officer of that name. What we refer to as wild horses in America—mustangs—are descendants of the Spanish horse brought to Mexico by Cortes. The genus also includes the ass, of which there are two

Wranglers on the set kept a constant supply of horses ready to be used as stand-ins for Pilgrim and other featured horses in the film.

species, and three species of zebra. All three can be interbred, but the offspring are sterile. Horses, zebras, and asses thrive on the rivers of grass that stretch across parts of Africa and South America in the Southern Hemisphere, and in the grasslands of America, Europe, and Asia in the Northern Hemisphere. The Tibetan wild ass lives at 16,000 feet. They are large, reddish colored and travel in small groups between Ladakh and eastern Tibet, and guard themselves with a sentinel donkey that alerts the others of danger.

Fifty-eight million years ago, *Eohippus,* more properly known as *Hyracotherium,* the first ancestor of the horse, roamed the earth. He was a rabbitlike animal, twelve-inches-tall, with four-toed front feet and three-toed hind ones. Slim and agile, it had an arched neck, straight back, and long tail, and lived in swampy areas. The fossils of Eohippus have been found in Suffolk, England, and parts of Europe, in Texas and the Big Horn Basin of Wyoming, but it was in North America where it flourished for another 20 million years.

As continents began to pull apart, climates cooled: semitropical cycads and palmetto forests changed into grasslands and savannahs, and the ancestral horse changed, too. In the Cenozoic era, Eohippus evolved into Mesohippus and grew to the size of a wolf; his middle toe grew bigger, almost a hoof.

Twenty-eight million years ago, Mesohippus became Merychippus and grew to be the size of a Shetland pony. His high-crowned teeth made it easy to eat grass, and finally his toes became hooves.

When the land bridge between Alaska and Siberia existed, the horse walked to Asia. That journey saved it: in the late Pleistocene era, the horse became extinct in North and South America along with other grazing and browsing animals—the camel, bison, and giant mastadon. On the flowing grasslands of Mongolia and northern China the horse flourished. The horse's legs lengthened and its sidetoes were lost, and it lived longer. A million years ago, it evolved into what we know now as the modern horse: *Equus caballus.*

During the Paleolithic era horses were hunted for food, but later became domesticated, long after the ox, sheep, goat, ass, and camel were, by nomadic tribes of central Asia. Riding a horse predated the wheel. In China, horses were used to pull chariots between 1765–1123 B.C. and were first ridden there shortly before 300 B.C. Mongolians used felt pads fitted over wood and leather rubbed with sheep's fat for a saddle. On these, Mongolian horsemen put together the largest contiguous empire the world has ever known. It wasn't long before the horse had gone almost all the way around the world, from the steppes of central Asia to the Middle East, North Africa, and Europe. Thousands of years later, the horse finally reappeared in North America, having come the long way around.

Horses caught rides to North America from both north and south. Five hundred years before Columbus set sail, the Vikings, who had already settled

In his first meeting with the troubled Pilgrim, Tom Booker makes his assessment.

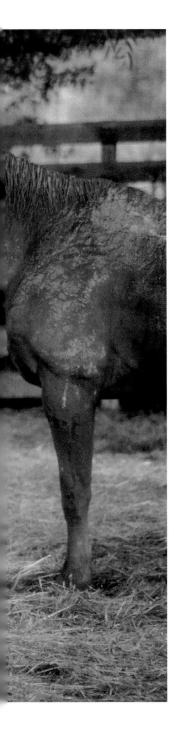

in Iceland and Greenland, explored the coast of New England and settled at L'Anse aux Meadows, Newfoundland, and probably brought with them the first cattle and horses to set foot on this continent. Under the Spanish flag, Columbus transported horses to the West Indies in 1494. Soon a steady stream of horses appeared: Cortes brought sixteen stallions and five mares to Veracruz, Mexico, and De Soto landed horses in Tampa Bay, Florida, in 1538. Gradually the North American continent was being repopulated by an animal that had once flourished there. How ironic that in Texas and Wyoming, *Equus caballus* ran over the fossilized bones of its ancient ancestors.

The horses brought to western America and used by vaqueros, Native Americans, and cowboys were in their early years descendants of two North African breeds, and a horse from Scandinavia called a jennet. What resulted was a horse unmatched for stamina, intelligence, resourcefulness, and speed.

When Islamic invaders, the Moors, conquered Spain in 711 A.D. they rode small, tough North African horses that came from two strains: the Roman-nosed barb and the dish-faced Arabian. Later mixed with the slightly larger dun Norse horse and a renewed infusion of barb blood, the Spanish began developing a

Scarlett Johansson with High Tower.

The pond used here was built especially for the movie by Jon Hutman. Having learned that horses don't like to be surrounded by straight banks, Hutman was sure that there were none in his pond. The bottom was lined with carpet and rubber to help secure the horses' and actors' footing. Greensman Phil Hurst planted the foliage surrounding the pond. After the scene was finished, the area was restored to its original state.

Like the accident scene in the beginning of the movie, the pond scene, where Tom Booker performs physical therapy on Pilgrim, was a difficult one, requiring several horses and days of shooting.

breed at stables in Cuba, Puerto Rico, and Santo Domingo that changed the face of North America. The horses were eventually called the Andaluz mustang. It had a straight nose, bright eyes, high withers, a short back, and small ears, and was often dun-colored with a black stripe down the back, or black, or piebald with a roan coat.

As vaqueros began settling along the Rio Grande in the 1640s, the Native Americans near Spanish settlements such as Santa Fe learned to ride and take care of horses. They had always been nomadic, moving with the herds, but it was dogs who had pulled the travois. Now dogs were replaced by horses.

In 1719, Pawnee villages had approximately one horse per person, but before 1735 there were no horses in the north or east of the Missouri River. Soon the Comanches, Apaches, Osages, as well as the Pawnees, began taking horses from the Spaniards and from the growing number of feral horses loose on the range. Once Native Americans were horseback, Spanish colonists lost the edge on their northward expansion.

The gift of the horse slowly moved up the latitudes. Southern tribes passed on horsemeat to northern tribes, and the Shoshonis, Flatheads, and Nez Perces passed horses on to the Blackfeet, Crow, and Lakotas, and on and on, until the horse became the center of southwestern and Plains Indian cultures.

It's hard to imagine what the first Indian who saw a horse and rider thought. To climb onto a horse for the first time and gallop out must have made him feel as if a curtain had been lifted and the universe suddenly expanded. He could go ten times farther in a day and ten times faster. The imaginary leap to the winged horse makes perfect sense: to get off one's feet, high

Previous spread: After being startled by the ring of Annie's cell phone, Pilgrim bolts off into a nearby pasture. Inset: Redford confers with, from left, Richardson, Joe Reidy and script supervisor Tom Johnston.

Above: After many hours, Pilgrim finally allows Tom to lead him out of the pasture.

off the ground, and effortlessly ride fifty miles a day across open country was to have become winged.

Horses revolutionized the lives of the Native American. The horses were used for hunting buffalo and other game such as elk, deer, and antelope, for carrying and pulling tepee poles, clothing, and supplies, and for staging little wars. The horse mobilized Native Americans geographically and economically: they could move faster and farther, which meant hunting was made much easier. For the first time, they had leisure hours. This new sped-up life was so appealing, some tribal people quit agriculture and went back to being hunter-gatherers again. And why not?

On the other hand, it put them face-to-face with other tribes. There were skirmishes, and horse thievery was epidemic, though the number of horses taken had more to do with establishing status and wealth than with the need for more horsemeat. Unlike the Mongolian horses, mares were not used for milk, and except in times of famine, horsemeat was not eaten. Horses were used for hunting and transportation only, but because they had opened the world up to the men and women previously on foot, they became the pride of any tribe that possessed them. One Comanche hunter thought that the Great Spirit had made horses just for his tribe.

Native Americans began riding horses long before the cattlemen took the herds north. Native Americans were horseback by the 1640s. There were so many feral horses around—herds of 200,000 horses could be seen in Arizona

A crucial point in the healing of Pilgrim: for the first time, the horse allows Tom to touch him physically.

Previous spread: Tom leads a horse up to the Creek House before asking Annie if she'd like to go for a ride.

Tom and Annie break into a full gallop across a field of wild flowers.

and New Mexico—that they didn't need to steal mounts from the Spaniards. The horses were there for the taking and no one cared.

As horses moved north, the Nez Perces in particular began breeding horses for both stamina and color. They favored the horses with a little white in their eyes, and speckled skin, whose hair was brown, red, or black-and-white: the painted horse and the Appaloosa. If the Euro-American colonists—the homesteader, gold seeker, and cattleman—had not streamed into the American West, it's said that the number of mustangs running wild on the open range would have rivaled the buffalo's—a number in the millions.

The Native Americans must have looked on in horror and disbelief as the mustang and buffalo herds were decimated by the cattlemen. Their genocidal violence was then aimed at the Native Americans—a story we all know. It reflected the inherent racist attitude of the northern European colonists toward both humans and animals: the small stature of the mustang meant they were inferior; the darker skin of indigenous people meant they were wild, intractable, and dangerous; and the natural communalism of wild animals with hunters and gatherers meant a society that could not be controlled.

The Native Americans wondered how the colonists could be so stupid as

Tom and Annie's horses enjoy
a break after their ride.

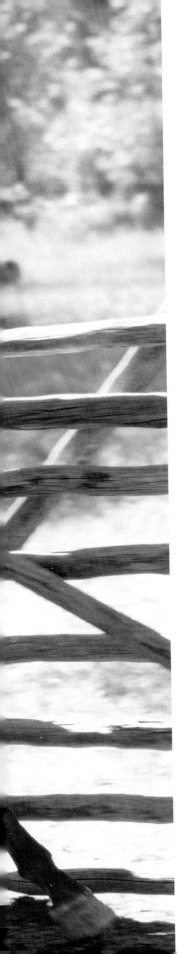

to supplant the buffalo, who had been adapted to open-range living, with the unresourceful, pampered cow. The bison came with built-in population control and naturally practiced short-duration, intensive grazing. They were able to paw through snow, and were bred and calved without management or help. These qualities were thrown over for the cow, who needed constant tending. And why would the cattlemen shoot the wild horses that, when mixed with the trail herds, broke open the snow cover with their hooves as the buffalo did, enabling the cattle to get to grass in the winter?

Soon enough the bison were gone, the Native Americans were lied to, dispossessed, and contained in vastly reduced acreage, and the mustang, with its quick intelligence, barrel chest, and hard feet—the only horse in North America able to run all day—was gravely reduced in number. Almost as soon as the open range was recognized as such, it ended.

In the meantime, ranchers began tinkering with their horses. In Oregon, draft horses—Clydesdales—were bred to cow ponies, resulting in a big-boned, short-backed horse with a calm, affable personality called the Oregon Lummox. In Montana and the Dakotas, Percherons were bred to mustangs and the offspring were called the Percheron Puddin'-foot. Californians developed, among other horses, the palomino, whose origin (which may be apochryphal) is said to be from a mission-owned horse, cinnamon-colored with a white mane and tail, bred to a Spanish barb.

Some ranchers wanted more handsome steads. Stallions and mares were brought from Kentucky by rail and bred to the Spanish *caballos*. In 1853 Richard King put together the King Ranch, a huge ranch in Texas still in existence today. It was one of the outfits where the quarter horse got its start in the West, though the breed's beginnings were in Virginia and the Carolinas.

King brought livestock up from Mexico—longhorns and mustangs. At one point he had 10,000 head of cattle, 20,000 head of sheep, 2,000 head of brood mares, and 100 head of saddle horses. He and others in Texas and New Mexico started breeding Kentucky thoroughbred stallions to the Andaluz mustang mares. Their progeny had names like Copper Bottoms, Cold Decks, Kentucky Whips, Printers, Steel Dust, and Billy Horse. These became some of the foundation horses for the breed.

The quarter horse was the first deliberately bred horse in the country and is still famous for having "a lot of speed, stamina, heart, and a lot of cow." That is, a horse that will give you its all, is athletic, willing, and has an inbred ability and passion to work cattle.

Gradually, the horses brought by the Spanish, themselves interbred three

Tom rides Pilgrim around the corral after saddling him up for the first time—another small victory in the recovery process.

Tom uses a flag to get
Pilgrim's attention.

ways and descended from the durable Asian pony, became diluted. But life is change. As one old cowboy said, "You can't go around saying this horse is good and that one's bad. Hell, they're all good. They're so good, we barely deserve to have them."

When asked what he liked best about horses, one friend, who has raised and ridden quarter horses for fifty years, said, "The smell." Then he laughed. "I guess you need more than that, don't you? It runs so deep. I just feel something missing when I'm not with them, and it gets restored when they're around. There's more, too: their innocent self-absorption just tickles me, and their calm acceptance of whatever happens to them, and the free way they move."

When there were tens of thousands of wild horses roaming the range, horsebreaking was a crude affair and remained so until recently. A horse was roped out of the remuda, his front legs hobbled, his head tied to a snubbing post in the middle of a round corral. Then he was "sacked out," meaning that the cowboy would wave gunny sacks at the horse, but since he was tied to the post, all he could do was struggle in terror. Then a saddle was thrown on and the horse cut loose in the small corral. He ran, snorted, bucked, reared, pawed,

Below: Tom tosses a lariat at Pilgrim's flank. As Brannaman says, "[It's] just to rattle his cage a little . . . not to scare him but give him a little push."

Tom Booker is not only a "horse whisperer," but a rancher as well. At left, he moves cattle before the branding, and right, he moves them into the high pasture for the summer.

and kicked. The young horse was roped again, a bit put into his mouth, and a young cowboy climbed on. Off they went, running and bucking out across the hills. "The whole idea was to break the spirit of the horse with fear and dominance so he would let a man ride him," one old cowboy reflected. "It wasn't a very good way of doing things—roughly akin to beating the hell out of your wife and kids."

Something was wrong. We had loved, worshipped, and venerated horses for thousands of years, yet we wanted to break them, break their spirit, when the very thing we loved most about the horse was the sensation of freedom, union, and harmony he gave us while riding him.

The name "horse whisperer" comes from an ancient source. There were certain gypsies who had a way with horses and could train them by whispering. That's all it took for Nicholas Evans to begin research for his novel. He came to America and stumbled on Buck Brannaman, whose work with horses was the inspiration for the novel from which this film was adapted.

Buck Brannaman and the teachers from whom he learned, Ray Hunt and Tom Dorrance, do not resort to dominance and submission, terror or restraint. "Always before, working with horses was a true grit kind of thing," Ray said. He started fifty years ago on a northern Nevada ranch, with a horse named

Hondo that no one could touch, much less ride. "I think I'd looked at too many Charlie Russell paintings. And I'd been getting by. Hondo taught me that getting by wasn't good enough. This was a life and death deal. I knew if I couldn't earn his trust, he'd kill me."

Buck Brannaman started working with young horses when he was only twelve. He had been taken from his father and sent to a foster home. Shortly thereafter he discovered Ray Hunt at a horse clinic and set about to learn his trade.

In *The Horse Whisperer,* Pilgrim is a troubled horse with a troubled owner, fourteen-year-old Grace. They have been in a terrible accident in which both were injured. Grace lost her leg; Pilgrim suffered deep chest wounds, as if his heart had been torn in two. From this trauma, horse and rider struggle to recover.

When the local veterinarians suggest that Annie give her consent to have Pilgrim "put down," they might well have said, "Let's put Grace down." Annie says no to the vets, and the journey begins: terror and self-hatred are shed, a marriage unwinds, a job is lost, love is ignited. The journey for girl, horse, mother, and trainer is not about true grit, but about true exposure, or in horse lingo, turning loose.

Self-discovery often comes through healing—for any animal, whether horse or human. When Tom Booker enters the dark stall with Pilgrim and finally urges him out into the light, we understand at that moment what "horse whispering" is about. These aren't instructions about getting a horse to do what we want it to do. Rather, they are life lessons about patience, dignity, respect, self-discipline—not just for the horse but for the human, too, for Grace, Annie, and Tom, and for all of us. It's about walking out from the dark corners and surrendering to the light, about making peace with things and coming alive again.

The first time Tom Booker approaches Pilgrim in a darkened stall, the horse rears, strikes, and bellows. "This is a normal reaction," Buck tells me. "The horse has been hurt and he's terrified. This is his way of talking, of saying "'Please don't hurt me again.'"

Buck Brannaman, who learned from Ray Hunt, who learned from Tom Dorrance, says, "When the mind is troubled, the body is troubled, and a horse never forgets. He may forgive, but he never forgets. That's why Pilgrim behaves the way he does. It's not meanness, just self-defense. In his position, we would do the same thing."

These remarkable men who work with horses remind us of the golden rule. They look into the horse and the horse tells them what it thinks through its actions and reactions. But if the human puts himself in the horse's place, in the horse's mind, then we'll know what to do. If Pilgrim is terrified and trying to protect himself, then we must foster trust and confidence. The smallest

Top and Bottom: Chris Cooper as Frank Booker and Ty Hillman as his son Joe in their first scene on camera. Center: Annie and Smokey, played by Don Edwards, look on as Tom Booker works with Pilgrim.

Pilgrim rears up before
being moved into the pond.

Right: Buck Brannaman
works a horse—notice
no one's feet are
touching the ground!

Head Trainer Rex Peterson shows off his prized trick horse High Tower.

With patience and determination, Tom Booker
uses all of the techniques of a horse whisperer
to get through to Pilgrim.

change, the slightest try—that's what we have to look for, and we must let the horse know that we've seen it.

If Pilgrim only wants to escape, then we have to learn to offer friendship without conning him, without trapping him, always giving him the dignity of escape. We have to learn to let up on the pressure we put on a horse, these horse whisperers tell us. We have to make an offer and step back so the horse can take it—or not—on its own terms.

Tom snaps the halter rope against the slats of the stall. The horse whirls and retreats deeper into the shadows. He wants to become invisible, to be dead. The remedy is action: Tom snaps the rope again and the horse runs by, out of the stall into a sunlit corral.

Out there, the horse takes a deep breath and snorts. Tom kneels down and looks into the horse's eyes, at his wounds and scars. The horse's withers twitch. He's uncomfortable and unsure. He wonders if the man will hurt him. Yet he looks at Tom. Curiosity is taking the place of fear.

"The whole idea is to get the horse to turn loose. Of his fears and his feet,

Frank and Diane Booker look on as Tom works with Pilgrim.

of his energy and ours," Buck says. Tom throws a pebble up into the air. "Look at me," Tom is saying to Pilgrim. Pilgrim stands quietly. That's enough for the day. Tom leaves.

A day later. Pilgrim is brought to the Double Divide. The corrals and round pen used for working with horses are under the shade of towering cottonwoods and pines. Dappled light falls on Pilgrim's back. He and Tom stand some distance apart. As Tom slowly approaches, Pilgrim is paralyzed with fear. Tom waves his lariat at the horse and the horse nervously moves around, going this way and that, trying to escape. Every time Pilgrim slows, Tom waves the rope to get him moving: he's directing the life in the body of the horse; he wants the horse to get comfortable within himself, to move out from under his own terror, to stop reacting and start moving freely. By turning loose with his feet, he drops his fear.

Tom works with Pilgrim, trying to get him to "hook on." When he tosses the coils of the lariat at the horse's flank, it's "just to rattle his cage a little," Buck tells me. "Not scare him, but to give him a little push." Pilgrim moves out. His shoulders, rump, and neck muscles smooth and flatten. There's life in his legs and feet; he's feeling more sure of himself, more confident about Tom.

"A horse gets scared and brave, sure and unsure, sick and well, full and empty, just like we do. I try to put myself in the horse's place," Ray Hunt told Buck many times. "When he stops being afraid he'll turn himself over to us." That's just what Tom Booker is doing.

"Hooking on," Buck says, "means drawing the horse to you. Getting him to find comfort and sanctuary with the human. What we did with Pilgrim is no different from what I do with a colt. I'm just fixing it up so that together, there can be trust."

In the film, Tom gets Pilgrim moving around the perimeter of the corral. All Pilgrim knows is escape. He's running. But he can't go far. Tom throws a wide loop over the horse's head that lands gently on his shoulders. It frightens him at first, and Tom applies pressure to the rope—not jerking, just a steady pull that says, "Come over here." It's an invitation, not a rebuke. He's trying to untrack the horse's hindquarters, trying to get him to stop bracing himself so that he can move smoothly and enjoy being alive.

Watching the footage, Buck says, "When the horse stops, you stop for a moment. You let him soak. You don't scare him or demand too much. If he doesn't hook on, you step back and let him keep traveling, but keep offering friendship. Then, when he stops again, see if you can't draw him to you. I don't mean pinning him to the fence or trapping him; it's pulling him off the fence with an invisible rope, and pretty soon, he comes."

Tom exerts a bit of pressure on the horse—not jerking, just pressure to stop, turn, and come to him. As soon as Pilgrim finds that opening, Tom

Redford with technical advisor Buck Brannaman.

releases. It's like a deep sigh, as if someone had opened his door to a starving stranger and said "Welcome." Pilgrim knows this. He stops and turns. Tom approaches. Slowly and gently, Pilgrim allows Tom to remove the rope from around his neck.

From that moment on, things smooth out between Pilgrim and Tom Booker. Tom ponies Pilgrim in a grassy pasture, moving like a lion. "He's learning to be a horse again," Tom says, smiling. Tom gently places the loop of his lariat over Pilgrim's head, slowly pulling down. Tom gets on his knees, as if to say, "If I can surrender to friendship, then you can." Pilgrim gives in to the pressure and drops his muzzle onto Tom's arms.

Ray Hunt says about those moments, "You have to look inside an animal to see where the harmony is. It's not a miracle. It's just there and you have to bring it out."

In the morning Tom swims Pilgrim in a water hole: physical therapy. The support and balance of the water help relax the horse. But Annie's cellular phone rings, scaring Pilgrim. He lurches; Tom calms him. But at the last moment, Pilgrim is seized by fear and a bad memory, and he bolts. "Let him go," Tom says. The horse must always be allowed the dignity of escape.

Tom walks out after the horse with miles of open country ahead of him. At a critical distance, Tom hunkers down in tall grass and waits. "It has to be the horse's idea to come back," Buck says. Tom waits all day. At dusk, Pilgrim gives in; his face is relaxed and his ears are up as he comes to Tom. Sanctuary. True unity. Willing communication. A friendship has been sealed.

Nothing Tom Booker has done is out of fear or aggression. He has not made it a contest with the horse. Only an offering. "It has to be a willing communication," Ray Hunt reminds us. "You fix it so he can try, then you allow him to work it out. If it doesn't work the first time, you keep trying. You never put a time limit on things. The soft spot is always open inside him; he just has to find it; he has to make it his own idea."

Near the end of the film when Tom ropes a foot back and uses it to lay the horse down, he's asking Pilgrim to take one more step: to accept Grace. But Pilgrim is still afraid. In the round corral again he runs, dragging the roped foot. "I sometimes have to lay them down so I can pet them all over. So they can smell and feel me and I can touch them," Buck explains.

The moment for Grace and Pilgrim to reunite comes. "You have to do this," Tom Booker insists as Grace walks across the pen. Pilgrim twitches. The dark corners are being exposed; light is being thrown on them and it's painful.

**Tom constantly challenges
Pilgrim to accept him.**

In order to ready Pilgrim for Grace, Tom
hobbles Pilgrim's front left foot. Finally, he
lays the horse down so Grace can stroke him.
This allows Grace to earn back Pilgrim's trust.

Grace's parents, Annie and Robert, look on anxiously as Pilgrim limps around the corral. It is difficult to watch, but Tom assures them the horse is not in any pain.

"You've got to do this," Tom keeps insisting to both of them. Down on the ground, Grace starts rubbing Pilgrim with her hand—his neck, legs, stomach, back, rump—over and over. Gently, Tom removes the foot rope: A softness goes through the horse's body, and through Grace's. She puts her foot in the stirrup. The horse rises to his feet with Grace on his back. He's not afraid, nor is she. He trots and lopes around the corral, smooth, relaxed, unbothered. Grace laughs delightedly. They're part of each other, like mane and tail. They're free.

An anxious Grace mounts Pilgrim for the first time since the accident.

THE MOVIE

Touchstone Pictures' *The Horse Whisperer* takes place on a family-owned cattle ranch called the Double Divide, in southwestern Montana. It is a story that starts with tragic losses—an accident that injured and traumatized a young girl and her horse, aptly named Pilgrim. Grace Maclean, age fourteen, loses her best friend in the accident as well as her own leg. Her horse is so badly injured that even after he has healed, he turns mean. Grace's parents are busy, prosperous, and aloof. The accident brings the entire family to the brink of dissolution. As winter turns to spring, so also does healing occur. Annie, Grace's mother, a high-powered New York magazine editor, realizes that she must take drastic action if her child and the horse are to be saved.

Annie, played by Kristin Scott Thomas, searches for someone who can look into the mind of the horse, to reestablish trust and harmony. She finds that horseman in Tom Booker—played by Robert Redford—a third generation Montana rancher with a gift for "thinking harmony with horses." Booker is at first diffident and skeptical. He is a man who has also suffered loss and loneliness, and states his thoughts bluntly to Annie when she calls to see if he will help with her horse problems. "I help horses with people problems," he says, then hangs up.

Thus begins a journey—a pilgrimage, if you will—for horse, child, and woman, toward solace, healing, and finally, love.

Johansson stands with the director she affectionately calls "Booey."

Redford steps in to direct Kristin Scott Thomas and Dianne Wiest during the scene where they wash dishes together by the creek. Dialect coach Carla Meyer looks on.

The film begins in a New York winter. A blizzard breaks and two young girls ride their horses in rolling farm country through deep snow. There is the accident, then the decision to take the horse to "Mr. Booker," as Annie quaintly calls him. As mother and daughter wend their way west, pulling a horse trailer carrying Pilgrim, the country opens in sinuosities: roads wind through plains and mountains; rushing rivers pour from high alpine mountains to muddy valleys and oxbow through barely green meadows, as summer comes slowly to the Double Divide Ranch, where Tom Booker, his brother and sister-in-law, and their children work and live.

The change of seasons bespeaks a change of interior weather: Annie's armor cracks; Grace and Pilgrim begin to climb out of their mutual terror, self-destruction, and despair. As meltwater from the high mountains comes down in the spring, so a tenderness seeps into the lives of those living at the Double Divide. Booker's loneliness is invaded; Annie's cluttered days simplify; Grace smiles. As the mountains, streams, and wide meadows emerge from under winter's obdurateness, healing occurs: animals, land, and humans rally

Here Annie asks Tom how long it will take to heal Pilgrim. He tells her, "That depends on the horse."

In a crucial scene where Tom looks for information about the accident, Grace asks, "Are you afraid of anything, Tom Booker?"

and thrive as the days lengthen and the sun returns. Patience is learned, as is self-reliance. And the truth about pain—that it must be met head-on and endured—is accepted.

It's said that true healing means to become truly yourself. That's what happens to Annie, Grace, and Pilgrim, as well as to Tom, who has been harboring old wounds. The open space where distractions are minimalized, where there are no places to hide, becomes a mirror, one that instructs and nurtures them.

"A horse is a mirror. It goes deep inside the body. When I see the horse, I see you, too," Ray Hunt likes to say. In *The Horse Whisperer,* Pilgrim is the mirror not only for his own problems, but also for the troubled minds around him. Tom Booker would say, "A horse knows the human twenty to one. You don't believe it, do you? But it's true. He knows what's on your mind when you get out of bed in the morning. He knows all about you as you walk toward the corral."

ROBERT REDFORD AS TOM BOOKER

To work with the mind of the horse, Tom Booker has had to go deep inside himself. What he found there was sometimes painful. Perhaps Tom Booker's capacity to understand the horse, to see both the horse and himself in the mirror, so to speak, is that he has also been lost, unsure, and sick at heart. And because of that, he knows how to bring horses and humans back from the abyss.

Tom was once married to a cellist in Chicago; they split apart when he realized he couldn't give up the ranching life and she couldn't give up her musical gift and ambition. "I thought maybe she could come out here and teach music to school kids," he says, realizing how naive he once was. But the ranch would never be her home and Chicago would never be his. Geography splits us; love stays.

He moves back to the family ranch, a place that has passed through two generations of the Booker family. It's a working ranch, no frills. Tom's brother, Frank, is married with three children. Tom is an appendage—a loved one. He lives in a room upstairs and takes meals with his brother and sister-in-law.

The Creek House—a lovely log cabin where he once lived with his wife—stands empty. Until Annie and Grace arrive.

When Tom tells Grace that "there's no sense in looking for a reason why things happen," he is attempting to make peace with himself. But it's a sterile peace, kept by distancing himself emotionally from women, until he meets Annie Maclean. Alone in his study late at night, we see another Tom Booker: He looks scholarly and contemplative with his wire-rim glasses. When he plays a record, we're surprised by what we hear: a Beethoven cello concerto. We know he's still hurting. He's lost the love of his life and the world has gone blank. He gets by, but his eyes tell us of the unspoken grief inside.

When Tom takes Annie for a ride on horseback, a seam rips. Annie's presence nudges old memories into view, and he finds they're less painful. That's because he's falling in love with Annie. While getting her to "turn loose" and have fun again, Tom is, in effect, reminding himself to let go. A tacit understanding passes between them: They want each other, but they're not sure. There's a tentativeness. There's jeopardy. But love begets love. It wakes Tom

Redford, above left, as actor playing Tom Booker, and below, as director, conferring with Richardson.

Tom waits in the grass for Pilgrim to come to him after the horse has fled into the pasture.

Brothers Frank and Tom discuss Pilgrim's progress.

up from his somnambulism and rips Annie's armor apart. Just what Tom would say about what takes place between the human and the horse.

"In drawing the character," Redford said, "I was interested in a man who had simply, classically, in the western sense, come to terms with what he was given. And that it wasn't meant to be that he was to be married and have a family. He'd accepted those terms and was moving on with it and was basically not aware that he'd closed off on love himself."

Tom Booker is a modern hero—or maybe a very old-fashioned one. He's humble, self-effacing, and he has learned to turn self-destructiveness into a form of generosity. By saving a horse, he saves himself and another human, though he would always tell you, "I'm here for the horse." And he is. But we quickly learn that the horse represents all living beings.

KRISTIN SCOTT THOMAS AS ANNIE MACLEAN

When Kristin Scott Thomas was offered the part of Annie Maclean, she loved the fact that her character underwent such a tremendous transformation during the film. Annie and Tom Booker couldn't be more opposite. As the editor of a fancy New York magazine, Annie Maclean has the exhausted impatience typical of some New Yorkers who think they live at the center of the world. Though she and her lawyer husband have a country house, she rarely seems to be there. Kristin Scott Thomas explains her character: "Annie's always been used to being in complete control of every single situation. Her driving force is to gain control, get to the top, and remain there."

As the British-born daughter of a diplomat, Annie has never had a real home; she seems incapable of grasping such an idea. It means nothing to her. She armors herself with work and being busy. There are no cracks into which a softness can enter; it's too psychologically dangerous for her to allow deep feelings or the complexities of a relationship to occur. Thus, a chasm grows between Annie and her kind husband, Robert, as does the gnawing tension with her teenage daughter, Grace.

Annie takes in the healed Pilgrim.

Tom helps Annie discover the playful side of herself again.

Scott Thomas continues, "I think that Grace's accident is never really accepted by Annie. She refuses to believe it, refuses to believe its impact on her life and on Grace's life." Yet, when the veterinarian, played by Cherry Jones, says about Pilgrim, "There's nothing that can be done for him," Annie refuses to let the animal be killed. What turns the screw in Annie's life is her native intelligence, as well as determination and drive. She understands that the welfare of the horse and that of her daughter are linked and inseparable. To save one, she must save the other. Ironically, her savvy about confronting daily problems at the magazine pushes her into the heart of the tragedy. And once moving toward it, there's no going back. But not without some bumps along the way.

First is Booker's refusal to help her; she solves that by going to him. Second is Grace's accusation that driving across the country pulling a horse trailer to see some cowboy is all for her mother, not for her or the horse. Maybe

Grace is right, maybe not. It really doesn't matter. What does matter is getting to Tom Booker.

Healing is too often associated with bandaging, sewing up, making a neat package of something messy. At the Double Divide Ranch, Annie learns that healing has more to do with letting things fall apart.

Spring comes slowly to the northern Rockies. Weather is capricious, nights are cold, the sky is multicolored, and the mud is deep. As the thaw comes out of the ground and the first haze of green grass can be seen, Annie's marriage begins to unwind—she can't even bring herself to invite her husband to Montana—and she feels herself drawn to Tom Booker. Yet she only shows impatience: "How long is it going to take, Mr. Booker?" she asks. "That depends on the horse," Tom says, meaning, when you want to get well, you get well. Annie loses her prized job. There's a narrow sense of liberation, yet she can't quite grasp what has happened to her. Her words "delayed shock" to explain her reaction to getting fired, describe her entire state of mind.

As the ground begins to thaw and Pilgrim's progress is substantial, Annie turns loose some things inside herself. She goes riding with Tom one day, and

Annie relaxes into the easy pace at the Double Divide.

In their final scene together, Robert tells Annie not to come home until she is sure about their relationship.

for the first time in years she enjoys the simple pleasure of being on horseback, and entertains the complexity and fascination of real love. But the territory of love is dangerous. Diane, Tom's sister-in-law, admonishes Annie: "Don't go looking here for whatever you're looking for. Don't make that man go through something it took him a long time to see his way clear out of the first time." Just as Annie gains some ground she loses it again. But that's what becoming your true self means.

SCARLETT JOHANSSON AS GRACE MACLEAN

In *The Horse Whisperer*, Grace Maclean has a picture-perfect life—private
school, weekend country house, horses, friends, and a loving father with
whom she is very close. In one hideous moment, all that is destroyed. She
loses her best friend, she loses a leg, she almost loses her horse, and the chasm
between her mother and father is revealed.

How does a young girl put so much back together? Why does death occur?
Why to her? How does healing occur? Why did she survive and not her friend?
These are Grace's burdens, the questions whirling in her head throughout the
film.

The young actress, Scarlett Johansson explains, "Grace is a very sensitive
character. She's fragile and you have to be careful not to take her sarcastic
humor as mean. She's from New York and she's very quick. She's smart but
hurt deeply. This film is about people building different relationships with each

other and trying to heal a variety of wounds. It's about people who are kind of renewing themselves, renewing their souls."

Pilgrim's trauma and disfigurement are also Grace's. Every action the horse makes comes from a desire to protect himself, to survive. The same with Grace—her sarcasm, her silences, her angry outbursts. Like Pilgrim, Grace keeps a critical distance from her mother and from a world that has senselessly harmed her. If she were Pilgrim she would strike, rear, and bite, too.

"There's no sense in looking for a reason why things happen," Tom tells her. And as all cowboys know, the only way to get over something is to get back in the saddle, no matter how long it takes. And Grace does. She's a four-

Forced to use a cane after losing her leg, Grace is led away from the branding by Tom Booker.

teen-year-old with all the confusions of that age gnawing at her. To lose a leg, wear a prosthesis, and walk with a cane is, for any teenager who is acutely aware of self-image, almost too painful to bear. But at the Double Divide, no one minds that she's missing a leg. She's treated in a dignified, adult way and given challenges and chores each day, like everyone else. The only way out of despair is action.

When asked about how she prepared for this part of the role, Scarlett said, "No one can tell you what it feels like to lose a body part—it's something I imagine you never get over and I had to develop that from the dramatic part of myself. I had a meeting with an eighteen-year-old boy for the technical end of it. He showed me how to pick things up and move around with a prosthetic. The make-up artist Gary Liddiard would constantly remind me when I wasn't swinging my leg or moving appropriately."

Like Tom Booker, Grace has days when things go dark inside and she is not sure if she wants to live, but she has a bubbling intelligence. Sometimes it gets in her way: Thus, the sarcasm and anger result, but in the end it helps her.

Part of feeling at home anywhere is being given something useful to do. To find a niche in society, no matter how humble—sweeping streets or cleaning stalls will suffice. This is how a human "hooks on"—just like Pilgrim—by allowing oneself to be drawn out of hiding, by developing a tenderness toward oneself and others, and finding sanctuary, not threat, in their presence. Tom helps Grace "hook on": he teaches her to drive; he gives her daily chores to do.

All through the film there are skirmishes between mother and daughter. The mother has been absent too long; the daughter, who has given her allegiance to her father, can't believe she is loved by her mother. Now mother and daughter are thrown together. Scarlett had never met Kristin Scott Thomas before shooting the movie. She says, "It was hard to jump into being mother and daughter when we had never met, but I think it actually helped in some ways because Annie and Grace are supposed to be uncomfortable and distant towards each other throughout most of the film."

To make things worse, Grace is fully aware of the attraction between Tom and her mother, a relationship that painfully excludes her. A crisis erupts. When Annie asks Grace why she won't talk, Grace responds, "Stop pretending like you care!" A heated conversation ensues. From Grace's point of view, she's the

Grace spies the troubled Pilgrim through the slats of his stall.

Johansson enjoys a break with her riding double, at right, and Patrick Markey's niece, Katie Risner, at left.

maimed and imperfect daughter of a mother who will accept nothing less than perfection. When the anger falls away, Grace and Annie make their way slowly toward each other. From Pilgrim and Tom Booker they learn this lesson: to relax with things as they are, that only unconditional love, or as close as you can get to it, will do.

As for Scarlett, six months after shooting, she still has fond memories of her time on the set. Scarlett said about working with Redford, "Booey [her nickname for Redford] had this technique to help me find my place in a scene, since we would sometimes shoot out of sequence. He would retell parts of the story, to help me guide my emotions." And as for shooting in Montana, Scarlett says "it was amazing. I had all these ideas of what Montana was going to be like and it was completely different from what I had envisioned. The sky was huge which, growing up in New York City, I had never seen before."

SAM NEILL AS ROBERT MACLEAN

Robert Maclean, played by the Australian actor Sam Neill, is a man who loves deeply: He loves Grace so much he can't give her the hard push she needs to get well; he loves Annie but doesn't get much in return. As he says about the character of Annie, "she has this kind of fierce intelligence and an unwillingness to compromise." Once they were young wanderers and fell in love while working in India. She stumbled upon him by mistake and was sent to rent a room at his house, and as sometimes happens while traveling, love ensues. Once they were close, but now there is no more chemistry and Annie buries herself in the enormity of her career.

"I think one of the central themes in the film is about a wounding and then a healing," Sam said while waiting to step before the camera. "It's about wounds healing. And for Robert, my character, the loss of his family, even the absence of his family, is like a limb taken away from him. It's as painful and as brutal and disabling as losing a limb. That's the central metaphor I worked with in *The Horse Whisperer*."

At their weekend house, seen at the beginning of the film, Annie seems never to appear. But Robert and Grace thrive there. They love being in the country with their animals. It quickly becomes clear that Grace is at the center of Robert's heart, not Annie.

Australian actor Sam Neill plays Robert Maclean.

From the beginning of the film, it is clear there is a special bond between Grace and her dad.

When the accident occurs, Robert is there first; when Grace learns to walk with an artificial leg, he's her shoulder to lean on. But his love is too soft in the center; it's tinged with self-defeat and sadness. When Annie decides to take Grace and Pilgrim to Montana, Robert accepts his fate and docilely stays behind. It's a terrible loss, but he seems unable to do anything about it. He will be deprived of participating in his daughter's healing.

When Robert finally visits the Double Divide, near the end of the film, he stands at the edge of the round corral. He watches Pilgrim fight reality; he watches Grace finally get on Pilgrim, and something happens inside him. The horse is a mirror: Like Pilgrim, Robert tells Annie, he can either fight the way things are or accept them. He takes a position of strength this time—a truer reflection of the love he feels: He doesn't want her unless she is ready to love him again.

Six months after shooting, the character of Robert Maclean was still with Sam. He had this to say: "Six months on, my character seems so distant that I can barely visualize him. At the same time I know he was so close to me and I felt such empathy for him that I have no perspective at all. He is too near to focus. I'm certain at least that I warmed to his humanity and compassion, his ability to forgive and his capacity to love. I recognized his pain and his commitment, and I felt I knew his family. In all this, Redford was my teacher and mentor. I relished the land and sky of Montana, and the companionship of a wonderful cast. With Scarlett, who plays my daughter, I was pleased we had a natural ease from the beginning. And working with my friend Kristin is as rewarding and real an experience as any actor can hope for."

DIANNE WIEST AS DIANE BOOKER

When Dianne Wiest was chosen to play the part of Diane Booker, the film might as well have been subtitled Wiest Goes West. She had never been to the Rocky Mountains before, never been on a ranch or around horses. She said, "I'm sort of from the east, and my acquaintance with ranch life and Montana was pretty much confined to movies."

When the actress asked Redford how to prepare for her character, she was sent to meet Marie Engle, the woman who actually lives on the ranch where the film was being made. Dianne had an easterner's romantic appreciation of the western life: "It was amazing because all of a sudden the real thing was standing in front of me, the kindness of this woman, the depth of her feeling for the land, and the work she does daily with her husband, which is so hard and which they do with such devotion."

As Frank's wife, Diane plays the traditional role of mother, bookkeeper, ranch hand, and cook. Like most ranch women, she's efficient, frank, thought-

Dianne Wiest plays Diane Booker. Before the filming of *The Horse Whisperer,* Wiest had never been on a ranch.

Diane helps set up camp for the night during the cattle drive.

ful, and jolly. She has to be; any other approach to life would be sheer misery. When she suggests that she and Frank go to Morocco for a vacation, he replies that Branson, Missouri, is good enough. She's good-natured about his response: "When I met Frank," Diane tells Annie one afternoon during a picnic, "I never thought about anything but being a rancher's wife. . . . But I don't deny that there are times I wonder about things I won't have. . . . Maybe one day I'll get to Morocco. Maybe not."

Sometimes the limiting factors of ranch life can seem suffocating. Gender is less an issue than the surplus of work: there are hundreds of animals entirely dependent on you, there are children, there's bad weather, and all the things that go wrong every day that must be mended—ten calves with pneumonia, a cow with a sunburned udder, a broken-down pickup, five miles of fence in need of mending after the elk tear it down, an irrigation ditch that blows out, a child who has the measles, the hired hand who quits. Typical day: an ungainly stream of mishaps and misadventures that never let up. Sometimes it's difficult to find a way to take a breather. Too many ranchers don't get away at all; the disburdening effect open space can have is reversed and becomes claustrophobic. As Marie Engle put it, "You choose this life."

CHRIS COOPER AS FRANK BOOKER

If Dianne Wiest had her first taste of the West through *The Horse Whisperer,* Chris Cooper, who plays Frank Booker, is a westerner who moved to New York because of his acting career. He was a natural for the film and relieved to come west again. Cooper grew up on a ranch in Kansas. "When I first went to New York," he recalls, "it literally took me two weeks to step out of my apartment. And I think that goes hand in hand with the armor you put on to survive urban life. You always have to have your antennae up in a place like Manhattan. When I come to a location like the Double Divide, it's a huge release for me. But of course, this has its own realities to contend with, too. You use other kinds of armor here."

Chris Cooper is a natural for the part and he looks it. As Frank Booker, he's quiet and happy to be on the ranch. World travel is not for him and he looks upon Annie's peregrinations with some horror. He's had to adjust to living and working with a brother who is gifted, and as they say in small western towns, "different." Countless ranches have been broken apart by brothers who can't get along. Or sometimes sisters. One set of sisters in Wyoming became famous for running a huge ranch together but never once speaking. They'd had a fight over water one day and went at each other with their irrigating shovels. After a stint in the hospital, they never spoke again, simply left messages for each other on a blackboard in the kitchen.

At the picnic following the branding, Frank is joined by real-life wranglers Curt and Tammy Pate.

Chris Cooper, who grew up on a ranch, plays Frank Booker.

THE BOOKER CHILDREN

The Booker children, a set of twins and eldest brother Joe, are typical ranch children. The twins are played by real-life twin brothers from local Livingston, Montana. Joe Booker is played by eleven-year-old Ty Hillman, a newcomer to the acting profession. But he has showbiz in him: he was discovered through the Colorado Junior Rodeo Association in which he competes in calf roping. To play the part of a rancher's son was no leap for him: "We brand every year just like the Bookers do; and the riding and roping, I do all that stuff," he said. But what he liked best about being on the set was learning rope tricks from horse trainer Buck Brannaman and stuntman Cliff McLaughlin. He said, "I knew how to do a couple of little tricks, butterfly and stuff. But now I can jump in and out. They've been teaching me a lot and it's been really fun."

Ranch kids are given responsibilities at a young age and learn to shoulder them easily. There are morning and evening chores to be done, dogs, horses, cats, and livestock to be fed, a 4-H steer to get ready for the county fair, a young horse to ride.

On the ranch, Joe's friendship helps bring Grace out of her shell.

Frank and Diane Booker's twin sons (at right), played by Austin and Dustin Schwarz of nearby Livingston, Montana, are fascinated by Tom's famous string trick (below).

Plus school. By the time they're fifteen they could run a ranch themselves. They've made long circles on horseback; they know that ranching is not "a simple life" and are physically hardened to living and working outdoors. That's why in *The Horse Whisperer* Joe seems older than Grace, though he's actually a few years younger. But the gap between them is bridged: He matches her city sophistication and street smarts with his wry wit and blunt way with words. He said, "He kind of gets her out of her shell. He likes her a bit, and I think that's the way I understand my character." For Grace, Joe is a breath of fresh air. No hidden agendas there. Joe is Joe and he welcomes her, leg or no leg, fear or no fear.

DON EDWARDS AS SMOKEY

Smokey, the hired hand on the Booker ranch, is played by the western singer Don Edwards, who also sings in the film. A Texan, he's no newcomer to life in the saddle. In the film, Smokey is quiet and shy, and a kindred spirit to Tom Booker. He understands what Tom can do with a horse and the way he lives. "In real life, I'm a traditionalist, too," Don Edwards said. "My music shows it. I've been singing and working in the music business for forty years, but I'd never given acting a thought. To get a chance to work with someone like Robert Redford is just the epitome of where you could go. It was too beyond belief. I'm just a cowboy folksinger, you know, but that's what they wanted. It really was just amazing and still is to this day."

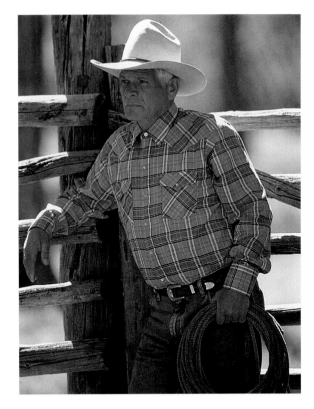

Real-life Western singer Don Edwards plays ranch hand Smokey.

Buck (above) was not only the technical advisor on the set, but also an occasional double for Redford. At right, he poses with Redford (far right) and Bernie Pollack (center), Redford's longtime costume designer.

This page, clockwise from left: T. J. O'Mara of the sound department at work on a John Deere Gator; Richardson making sure a shot is perfect before shooting; Richardson films Redford, Scott Thomas, and Johansson in a scene.

Left: Richardson poses with some of the crew, including members from extras casting, props, camera department, sound department, grips, assistant directors, gaffers, and video department.

Following spread: Richardson used this foliage-trimmed scrim to create the same shadow patterns and lighting for scenes shot over a number of hours or over a series of days, where the sun was constantly changing position. This helped ensure continuity in the scene.

ON THE SET

Landscape as character is an important element in *The Horse Whisperer*. The early scenes in the film were shot near Saratoga Springs, New York. It is big, rolling country with massive barns on the southeastern edge of the Adirondack Mountains. Deep winter brings cold and snow. Nevertheless, the company had to import more snow for the filming of the accident scenes. In fact, they made so much snow that they saved a local ice company from going into bankruptcy.

The resulting winter scenes are stunning. By turns sensuous, austere, and melancholy, a shadowy light falls over the snow, not menacing but tentative—a perfect mood in which to shoot the accident scenes. The Roosevelt Baths in Saratoga Springs State Park, currently undergoing restoration, were used for the hospital where Grace was taken after the horse falls with her.

From there, the company moved to New York City to shoot the Maclean family apartment. A museum in New York City was used as the exterior of Grace's school.

During a three-week hiatus to allow winter snows to melt, producer Patrick Markey oversaw the traveling shots of Annie, Grace, and Pilgrim driving cross-country while it was still spring, and the movie company began moving to Montana. "We were literally chasing the seasons for most of the schedule," Markey said. It was early June and unusually heavy snows were melting. The rivers were overflowing—right onto the set. Much of the Double Divide Ranch was under water. "We had to lay planks down and walk on them to get from one part of the set to the other without bogging down," Redford

Left: Grace and her best friend Judith, played by Catherine Bosworth, head out for a ride that ends in the tragic accident that sets the film in motion.

Below: From left, Rex Peterson, High Tower's trainer, head wrangler Mike Boyle, and High Tower on the set in upstate New York.

Below right: Redford confers with Philip Pfeiffer, 2nd unit director of photography (New York), on location near Saratoga Springs.

said. "The floods caused a lot of hardship for the crew. They were building in knee-deep water and shooting in knee-deep water. But there was one payoff, and that's the beauty of the skies because of the storms. It rained and rained, but when it cleared the skies were magnificent—red and pink hues and towering thunderclouds.

"You know that scene where I first meet Annie?" Redford continued. "You'll notice that it was a medium shot—from the waist up. That's because we were standing in knee-deep water. When I walked over to her, you could hear water sloshing. Every time the crew sees that scene they start laughing."

The set designers had their hands full sandbagging the houses. "We worked for three weeks in waders," Brian Markey, the head carpenter said. Then the mosquitoes came on. "You'd look down and you couldn't tell if it was your arm or not. Any part of your body that was exposed was a moving mass of mosquitoes." Crew members wrapped everything, including themselves, in mosquito netting, but it was still miserable. The mosquitoes persisted into September, trying everyone's patience.

The truck Redford used was a '77 Ford pickup he had spotted on a street in Livingston. He dispatched someone from the crew to purchase it and use it as Booker's truck in the film. The couple who sold it to him said it had been

Annie at an editorial meeting for *Cover Magazine* where she is the editor-in-chief.

Opposite: Annie and the veterinarian, played by Cherry Jones, examine the troubled Pilgrim after the accident.

Following spread: Annie heads west with Grace and Pilgrim.

their wedding gift to each other twenty years before, but the price was right and it would be in a great film, and so, why not?

Since the Double Divide is a cattle ranch, its work went on alongside the film crew's. Cattle were moved, alfalfa irrigated, and hay was baled and stacked. Two women from the ranch appeared in the picnic scene, but the happiest member of the Engle family was one of the working cow dogs who discovered the catering tent. He became a permanent fixture there.

Redford observed that "this film, for me, provided the opportunity to show the West not only as it was—as a way of life—but as it still is in very, very small

Preceding spread: Using a scrim to create the appropriate lighting, Redford sets the stage for a scene between Tom and Annie.

144

Diane and Frank Booker enjoy the picnic after the branding. To the right of Frank is trainer Curt Pate.

From left, Annie, Tom, Edith Engle, who works as an extra in the scene, and Tom's mother, played by Jeanette Nolan, settle in for a celebratory picnic after a successful branding.

Following spread: Tom finally earns Grace's trust. Here, they head out of the barn to take on the task of healing Pilgrim together.

pockets, where it is almost an anomaly. It was interesting to me to pick a family that still lives the way they lived a hundred years ago, where you farm your land, ranch your land to yield a crop that will sustain you."

"In the West, there's a different kind of closeness. Things tend to be understated because there's no time to sit around and jaw about how you're feel-

Diane warns Annie "don't go looking here for whatever you're looking for."

Previous spread:
Robert arrives at the
Double Divide.

Below: After Grace
pleads with him, Robert
tells the story of how he
and Annie first met.

ing . . . it's as much the behavior and ethic of living—how you live in the West—as a philosophy that we tried to capture in the filming of *The Horse Whisperer.*"

By all accounts, the filming of *The Horse Whisperer* was a special experience for everyone involved—undoubtedly because of the powerful nature of this story set amid some of the most beautiful country in the world. This is a film that called on the expertise of not only the finest actors and filmmakers in Hollywood, but also the best wranglers and horse trainers. *The Horse Whisperer* provided a unique opportunity for two seemingly disparate worlds to come together and tell a story that is as much about the landscape as it is about the people and animals who live there.

Above: Annie and Tom share a dance.

Right: In one of their final scenes, Annie and Tom come to the painful realization that they cannot remain together.

PHOTO CREDITS

Photos by JAY DUSARD appear on the following pages: 2, 3, 4, 13 (top), 14, 15, 34, 35, 78 (inset), 142, 143 (full and inset), 158, 159

Photos by JOHN KELLY appear on the following pages: 1, 12, 27, 28, 29, 31 (bottom right), 32, 37 (bottom left), 38, 39, 41, 47, 48 (top), 49, 52, 54, 55, 57, 61, 74, 75, 76, 80, 84, 89, 95, 99 (top), 102 (bottom left), 119, 129 (top), 130 (top)

Photos by ELLIOTT MARKS appear on the following pages: 5, 6, 7, 8, 10 (full and inset), 11, 13 (bottom), 19 (top and botom), 21 (top and bottom), 23, 24, 30, 31 (top), 33 (top and bottom), 36 (top), 37 (top), 40, 42, 43 (top and bottom), 44, 45, 48 (bottom), 51, 58, 59, 64, 65, 66, 67, 68 (top and bottom), 69, 70 (full and inset), 71, 72, 73, 77, 82, 83, 87 (top, center, and bottom), 88, 90, 91, 92 (top and bottom), 93, 96, 98, 99 (bottom), 100, 101, 103, 104, 105, 106, 107, 108, 109, 110, 111, 112, 113, 114, 115, 116, 117, 118, 120, 121, 122, 123, 124, 125, 126, 127, 128 (top and bottom), 129 (bottom), 130 (bottom), 131 (top and bottom), 132, 133 (top, center, and bottom), 134, 135, 144, 145, 146, 147, 148, 149, 150, 151, 152, 153, 160

Photos by KEN REGAN appear on the following pages: 62, 136, 137 (left and right), 138, 139 (top and bottom)

Photos by BARBARA VAN CLEVE appear on the following pages: 16, 36 (bottom), 78, 85, 154, 155

All cover photos are by ELLIOTT MARKS

ACKNOWLEDGMENTS

This book would not have been possible without the generous help and hard work of the following people:

Robert Redford, Patrick Markey, Kristin Scott Thomas, Scarlett Johansson, Sam Neill, Dianne Wiest, Chris Cooper, Buck Brannaman, Jon Hutman, Brian Markey, Gretel Ehrlich, Katherine Orloff, Dennis Aig, Ray Hunt, Lois Smith, Jennifer Glaisek, Melanie Johansson, Bill Reynolds, Theresa Curtin, and Donna Kail

At Dell Publishing: Carole Baron, Diane Bartoli, Dorothy Boyajy, Mary Fischer, Leslie Schnur, Marietta Anastassatos, Anita Henry, and Johanna Tani

At RR Donnelley & Sons: Dave Delano, Matt Miller, Ron Heyman, Scott Meyers, and Marcia Lerner

At the Walt Disney Studios: Karen Glass, Holly Clark, Jonathon Garson, Paige Wright, Stephanie Harris, and Daniel Pensiero III

At Byron Preiss Visual Publications: Gilda Hannah, Kathy Huck, and Byron Preiss